Things Not Seen

Things Not Seen

―⁓

Eric Potter

RESOURCE *Publications* · Eugene, Oregon

THINGS NOT SEEN

Resource Publications
An Imprint of Wipf and Stock Publishers
199 W. 8th Ave., Suite 3
Eugene, OR 97401

www.wipfandstock.com

ISBN 13: 978-1-4982-2924-1

Manufactured in the U.S.A.   07/30/2015

To Sarah

Contents

III

Fight Fire with Fire | 35
The Worst Thing | 36
September | 37
Another Language | 38
Faith | 39
Entanglements | 40
Personal Economy | 42

IV

Wide Awake | 44
Rendering | 46
For Example | 47
Extravagance | 48
New Communion | 50
Tattoos | 51
Vegetables from my Neighbors' Gardens | 53
Blessed | 55

V
Icon Writing

Icon Writing | 59
Doors of Perception | 61
At the Burning Bush | 63
Christmas Card Icon | 64
Mothers and Sons | 65
Crying in the Wilderness | 66
The Business of Icons | 68
Favorite Saint | 69
Man of Sorrows | 71
At the Cross | 73
Breath | 75
Still Life | 76

Notes | 77

Acknowledgements

Saint Katherine Review: "Faith"

Stone Work: "Still Life"

Still Life. By Eric Potter. Steubenville, Ohio: Franciscan University, 2010: "Still Life"

I

Lament

I do not have the poet's ability
    to find God
        in a blade of grass,
            the silver

trail of a slug or a dove's
    plaintive song,
        to hear a prayer
melancholy   in the breath of flowers,

or see in the sunlight slipping
    through sycamores
        a sacrifice
            of praise.

The squirrels circuiting the neighborhood
    preach me no sermons,
        the rabbits nibble
            in non-liturgical silence,

and even the summer breeze,
    which blows where it will,
        has nothing to offer
            but unspirited sighs.

For me there is only the unweeded
    flower bed, the browning lawn
        in desperate need
            of rain.

When will the sky's endless
            blue seem more
                than natural?
                    When will I

taste and see what my brain
        claims and the creed
            affirms, a world
                aflame?

The Odds

The race is not to the swift
or the swallow. My money's on

the peregrine falcon
that can outpace NASCAR

in a nosedive. Impressive.
Until you start wondering

what exactly the point is.   *what one is able to*
Ability and utility ——>   *do vs. what is useful*

may rhyme but have no reason
to be together, like tying

a cherry stem with your tongue ——   *ability*
or dropping an atom bomb. ——   *utility*

Persistence, while admirable,
only makes you more lost

if it's in the wrong direction.
A trail can easily be confused

with a trial. What happens
in the middle makes all

the difference, so make
your best case and let

things run their course,
just another game of chance

in which, despite the fabulous
results of that tiresome tortoise,

you are, actuarially speaking,
better off backing the hare.

Certainty

Such ovoid and smooth
perfection can't feed you.
Nothing broken, nothing
gained. Like a cliché,
your brain simply
mirrors its surroundings,
hardly wider than a hand,
it comprehends so little.

[handwritten annotation: Cracking an egg?]

[handwritten annotation: We're the egg in God's hand?]

Matter of Fact

I guess there's a little
Herod in all of us,
fascinated and threatened
by the truth in equal measures,
not wanting to kill it,
but not wanting it
free to accuse us.
We'll tolerate most anything
to keep from being seen
as intolerant, and if it takes
an axe to silence
the voice of conscience
we'll gladly wield it,
serving up the tongue
of truth on the silver
platter of convenience.

History of Ideas

Whate'er my God ordains is right.
Whatever is is right.
Whatever is is.
Whatever is?
Whatever.

Meandering

The casual ramblings
of a pedestrian mind
will get you nowhere
intellectually.

Better to follow
the body's binary
code of pleasure
or pain,

hot/cold, hard/soft,
a simple Yes or No or
Yes, Yes, Yes, Yes.
No

need to be stuck
with the wandering stars
as if you're crossed
like lovers

whose Yes always collides
with a cosmic No,
while the gods, champions
of indifference,

continue their Olympic sport,
unlike the gold medal
runner who leaves nothing
to chance,

leaves everything behind
that might prove
an impediment to finishing
the course,

a simple case of mind
over matter, of focus
the way a magnifying
glass

gathers the mild sun
to make a point
so heated it can start
a blaze.

Conversation Piece

These dolphins don't tear
any gong-tormented sea,
they don't even swim,
they just cling together
on their magnetic base,
perfect gift for that someone
you don't care much about,
but don't hold that against
these die-cut metal bits
who mean no harm just want
to stick together and will
take whatever shape they're given.

Even the [?]
lines stick
together

If you stuck them in a poem,
you'd have to load them down
with lots of literary symbols,
about losing our grip
on the magnetic chain
or the way some hand is
always forcing us into
positions we'd never choose.

Or not

Boom, meta

And that would be absurd
since these dolphins aren't meant
for anything except to sit
on a desk, a conversation
piece or mindless game
to fill the empty time.

Sleeping Dogs Lie

Though you really shouldn't let them—
it's not good for their character,
and the world already has more falsehood
than it needs. You probably have more
than you need, all those little white lies,
omissions of detail, not to mention
your social smile, and the questions you ask
for form's sake, though nobody's knocking
forms, which don't really give society the lie
so much as define it, the way
hypocrisy lubricates social intercourse.
Whatever the case, we can expect more
of our dogs, knowing they're superior,
not just their sense of smell but their unconditional
love, though they're often just pretending
to sleep. Witness the way they leap
to their feet if you make the slightest move,
always on the lookout for a walk or a treat.

Arrowheads

My uncle gathered them from a fresh-plowed field,
he polished them and placed them in a box.
So strong the call of precious things concealed
one soon ignores the warnings and the locks.

My cousin and I would sneak them out and test
the once-sharp edges on our tender skin,
imagining if one should pierce our chest,
the untold damage it could do within.

Our covert operation drew us near,
as side by side we touched each artifact,
we felt a tremor, neither pain nor fear,
as if some secret place within had cracked.

We put away the box without a sound,
wishing those buried things had not been found.

If this page

is a field, then my mind is a butterfly,
one of the small white ones so common
in summer that flirts with one plant or another,
brushing a spiky green weed, breezing
past pale orchises, but never sipping
a drop of nectar or spreading a grain
of pollen through whole mornings of droning   → THE BLOCK
sunshine, of birds offering their singular
examples, unafraid of redundancy,   The notable/noteworthy
unselfconscious about taking a position   poets.
on branch or bush and pouring forth
what's on their mind, having something
in mind, their hollow bones filled   Or just confident
with such fullness they must release it   voices
into the air that accepts all voices   ———→ voices
without comment, knowing nothing
will last in a world where all things
pass, those flowers, that butterfly,
and summer mornings in this field of grass.

Reducing his poem
    to a mere field
        of grass.

15

September Sunday Afternoon

"Sorrow is my own yard."

Sorrow is the sun leaving long shadows
  on the lawn and lighting the tall oaks.

Sorrow is the endless blue of evening, a thumb
  of gray smudging the edge of sight.

Sorrow is goldfinches flaring from branch to branch,
  a ragged vee of geese, their stray
  cries floating to the ground.

Sorrow is the song of unseen birds
  who will soon fall silent, the stir
  of hidden limbs that will soon be seen.

Sorrow is the leaves shaking their heads
  at the air's innuendo or keeping   *HA!*
  their unwavering counsel.

Sorrow is the just-opened book, the preface
  and acknowledgements, the eloquent   *YES*
  first paragraph on history.

16

Dandelions

Your yellow stars could
constellate a galaxy
were you not so committed
to the terrestrial.
Though many have tried
to uproot you, you persist
in your dreams, setting
each one free to be
borne by the wind
like bold mariners
seeking the world's end,
or a place to begin.

II

California Dreaming

The airplane always lifts you out of local weather
and lets you down in a different clime.
After de-icing, we hurtled the snow-slick runway,
shouldered through the low clouds, and broke
into that higher altitude where everything seems clear,
where far below the earth lies quiet as a map.
All afternoon we chased the setting sun,
landing after dark in a place I'd never been.

Next morning I stepped into the scent
of something blooming in the dark,
first vegetation I'd smelled in months.
Down by the beach vapor lifted from an outdoor pool
where ghost-like figures gathered to swim laps,
and the palms swayed their gravity-resisting trunks,
like something out of Salvador Dali.
In the half-light, the surf washed ashore like gray slush,
and I waited for the sun to crest the rim
of the bowl-like mountain holding the town.

Later at a breakfast on that mountainside,
surrounded by the bare earth and blithe air
by bird song and the promiscuous green,
it was easy to know what I should think.
Amidst the blended notes of artists and academics,
listening to the poet who spoke of peace
in poem after poem, each one ordinary
and miraculous as a loaf of bread,
I could believe in shalom and might have

begun beating my sword into a plowshare.

I thought of home, the layers it takes to keep
off the cold, the voices I'd hear keen
as the wind chill, the scrape of branches,
wisps of snow lifting from the bare fields,
snow plows flashing past in the dark.

I wondered how you make peace
in such a world. I thought of my poet heroes,
whose courage I admired, whose words
I wanted to believe. How I envied
the clarity of their difficult convictions.

By afternoon my jacket had become an encumbrance.
Through the growing haze I glimpsed the ocean's gray shrug.
One more day and I would go back east where the snow
would last for months, where the home team would lose
its playoff game, and the airline my luggage.

Actually Speaking

Because actually rhymes with factually
some mistake its certainty for certitude
whereas it's more a matter of tone
and mood not in the grammatical sense
of verbs like predicate predict or prove
but in the sense of affect a confidence
that might be affected but whose effect
is acceptance which is not belief
exactly but borders on it proximity
approaching the limit which is
never equivalent but close enough
for calculating solutions to most equations
all things being equal that's good
enough in a crisis real or imagined
the latter always looming larger
in that *mundo* behind the eyes
where you write direct and play the lead
like any pro you have your con
some flimflam trick to dazzle
the crowd into giving you exactly
what you want a matter after all
of confidence not truth which isn't
what we were speaking of actually.

One sentence.

Flows through

FEELING freedom from doubt

FEELING

part of sentence
that expresses what is
said about the subject

As a verb: affirm, declare

MATH/SCIENCE

CETERIS PARIBUS

The mind

Where you get what you want, not the TRUTH...

NICE

23

Unable

He would not will
his keepsakes away,
though he didn't mind
us breaking down
boxes, loading
his truck with scrap
lumber, sweeping up
the dust and leaves,
trashing broken
tools and toys.

Still, he would not
let us touch
the jars of coins
he meant to sort
hoping to find
what's valuable and rare
or let us move
the boxes of papers,
so many reports
to type, so many
minutes left
to correct
and when we tried
he yelled at us
as if we'd sung
"amen" before
the hymn was done.

How silly we thought,
but left them there
for him to get to
if he would or could,
a gesture simply
meant to placate,
forgetting a plan
is always better
than despair.

Seamstress

At the dining room table,
where the sunlight, softened
by gauze curtains, shines
on the blue veins threading
her white hands, my mother
is sewing. Those hands,
stiff though not arthritic
like her mother's, unhindered
by the jeweled engagement
ring, guide the fabric,
the right fingertips nearly
touching the needle that
plunges up and down,
now fast, now slow, a tempo
known since childhood,
the left smoothing everything.

Remember the Hawaiian rainforest,
how everything felt overdone,
everything living for the moment,
all that prodigal green silk
embroidered with iridescent birds?

The creation

I want to know what demands
so much attention. The needle
darts in and out. You lift your head
like a deer disturbed while feeding,
but all you say is how much
you miss your father.

*A good man.
She misses / lacks
a good man.*

One True Sentence

Looking for one you can lock on
that can lock you in
for a morning for a lifetime
of leafing through a forest
hoping to recover the necessary
indolence barely distinguishable
from insolence a disregard of limits
that makes transgression impossible,
where freedom means elimination
of distraction and caution —
an off-road trek that will end
hopefully at illumination
while the player heeds the whistle
accepting the field the fact
of another game played between lines
a matter of receiving and sending
to him who wants it
who ardently desires to possess
with a goal certainly but with
unhurried finesse as pass by pass
the ball finds its way to the net.

27

Daffodils

This gift arrived
un-blooming,
a bouquet of green,
dormant in a glass
vase on our table.
A day's heat
for them to blow,
yellow explosions
frozen, symmetrical.
Beneath the trees
their unmodified
cousins arrive,
a bed of green
nails bursting
through the snow.

A Shooting Star

is neither
is merely
a lump
that's lost
its place
is falling,
its atmosphere
providing
enough
friction
for ignition
to consume
itself.

Squirrels

Not cute and cuddly
but bush-tailed bandits
you plunder feeders
break into attics

storybook creatures
bane of homeowners,
and paw the flower pots,
and badger blue jays.

Height-loving loners
sometimes you slip
and land on the lawn
brain stuff budding

who look so agile
in your frantic scurrying
where you lie twitching,
from your broken skull.   *Oh my.*

When hunger's specter
you gorge and gather
except at the end
you pertly punctuate

haunts you to harvest,
growing most restless
when like a gray exclamation   *YES*
the unmoving pavement.

Playfully peppering
chattering cheerfully,
so gleeful your gambols
are determined defenses

the snow with your prints,
you chase your neighbor
but those games of tag
of your private domain.

When returning robins
and flowers ignite
you're stuck with stores
and winter-honed hunger

wrangle fresh worms,
their fast-burning fuses,
grown stale
wanting harvest.

Breathing Room

Power shouldn't be confused with
charm, a warm hand on the shoulder
steering the heart past shallows.
To play with *non sequiturs* is not,
necessarily, to ply your trade.
Drop a beat and float on its rhythm.
Cast your bread on the water
and see what rises open-mouthed.
Everything demands your attention,
even the circus with its sad elephants
linked trunk to tail like the days
of the week on a forced march toward
Saturday's certain disappointments.
If you wake up lost in the error
of "would," if you can't make sense
of anything, try making music, though
the principles of harmony elude you,
try to elide duty and desire,
the way dandelion and daffodil
are simply a matter of perspective,
their charming flags still powerless
against the world's sensible green.

Fight Fire with Fire

Everybody knows a coyote will
gnaw its foot to free itself,
though some claim it's fear
that drives the beast to worry
the limb till it breaks clean off.
Whether foresight or frenzy
with the offending member gone,
the creature's free to move on
like those movie spies
who refuse to possess anything
they can't leave behind
or that guy pinned by a boulder
facing a slow and certain death,
who amputated his own foot—
too clean a word for the hack job
performed with his pocket knife
un-drugged and hardly sterile—
then dragged himself to his truck.

What would you do
faced with certain death,
soon or late, fast or slow,
how much would you be
willing to sacrifice?
Could you sever a limb
to save your skin,
would you even want to
just to get back
to this world, this life?

The Worst Thing

about being raised from the dead
wasn't returning to the body
with its shortness of breath
and daily need for food and rest,
wasn't disappointment at the ordinary
daylight illuminating nothing
but the drab village, a landscape dull as dust,
it wasn't even knowing everything
would have to be gone through again—
the wasting of disease and sorrow
of friends, the pain and fear
(less now, perhaps), the last breath.
No, the worst was everyone else,
people I'd known my whole life
struck dumb in my presence,
a few tried to pass the time with weather,
or shook their heads at rumors
the authorities wanted me dead
but most just stared while the news spread
like a fever till I couldn't move without a crowd
dragging behind me like a bad leg.
Eventually, I stopped going out
but they breached the gate and stormed
into the courtyard to call me forth
overrunning everything, even my prize lilies
the ones I'd spent a lifetime cultivating.

September

On every tree and bush, the earth-
heavy leaves darken and curl.
Dust coats the weeds along the gravel
road to the pond, coats the pond itself
where the first frail leaves sail
like bright boats then disappear.
The thoughtless sky offers nothing
but the sun's pale wine and summer's
heat grown stale. Algae-brown
and only half full, the bird bath offers
its tepid pleasures to fat robins.
Acorns drop thicker than rain.
A garter snake weaves its checkered
length through the warp of grass
and disappears beneath the rhododendron.
The grass, crinkly as steel wool, scours
the children's bare feet. Habit-driven
homeowners drive their mowers,
stirring up dust but cutting nothing.
The geese leave early, shouting excuses.
Golden rod threatens to ignite the woods
and sumac smolders a dull red.
At the field's edge, doves powder
their gray feathers then fly off.
Yellow jackets, knowing their time
is short, move restlessly
among the shriveled windfalls.
Obscure among the brown weeds
a fox pants in the afternoon heat.

Another Language

My son is learning another language.
Me gusta queso, he says,
which may or may not be true.
He's reciting a script of sounds
his tongue must struggle to make
of shapes his brain must learn to take.

My son is learning another language.
Functions, he says, and derivatives,
eigenvector, aldehyde, bijection.
He says these lines so trippingly
yet even his explanations are sounds
I can't get my mind around.

My son is learning another language.
He forms each word as carefully as he can.
I smile and nod, watching his face
and hands as if he were a foreigner
whose meaning I might somehow guess
from this dumb show of gesture.

My son is learning another language,
a slow emigration to a country of his own.
It is what I've always wanted,
always feared. How do I say
"Farewell" in this brave, new tongue?
How do I say, "Well done."?

Faith

that stray dog, poking
its nose into everything,
turning up unannounced
and unwanted, distrustful
of crowds, always
loitering on the edge,
but never close enough
to pet, just a mutt
with bad teeth and worse
breath, limping along
half-wagging its stump,
no collar, no shots,
no registration,
won't roll over or fetch,
won't come when called,
though it may show up
at your back step
lean and hungry,
if you feed it table scraps
it might keep coming back,
if you chain it,
it might not stray again
but it won't be the same.

Entanglements

Like Schrödinger's cat
I'm here and not here
in ways you'll never
know but will learn
to live with, the way
you learned arithmetic
is for children, no solutions
in the back, everything
a matter of fractions
and you always trying
to live by half
measures, to solve
for x, unwilling
to accept a variable
means just that.
Admit to having no
more sense of direction
than a deaf bat,
be willing to board
a rudderless boat
where the salt air
will drown the scent
of land and the waves
the freeway's whine.
Finding yourself
at sea, you might
realize the box

is not a gift,
though you open it
again and again.

Personal Economy

I would not spend my life today
always thinking of tomorrow,
but give myself without delay,
so free I'd never have to borrow
future pleasures just to pay
the current balance of my sorrow.

Wide Awake

U2 at Heinz Field

Eyes closed I hear the voice
I've listened to for years.
This time it's live and the band
pumps out a sound that fills
the stadium and forms
the atmosphere we breathe.
I breathe the liquor breath
of sixty thousand fans
who are singing to the band
but cannot hear my wife
who is singing next to me,
can only feel her move
in her mysterious ways.
My voice lost in the sound
of the crowd, the throbbing bass
and drum and all our hearts
that beat and beat as one.

If I wanted to see, I could
look at the Jumbotron,
like watching a DVD,
but that's not why I came.
You're here in the flesh,
closest you've ever been
though still so far it's tough
to see from the cheap seats.

I know if I could leap
that gap and reach the stage,
you'd take me by the hand.

Instead, you elevate
our souls to dream of a place
where the streets have no name,
where all the colors bleed
into one, and all we can do
is go there with you hoping
tonight we can be one.

And you just play and play
right through a fourth encore.
The crowd is heading home.
It's late, but I'm not sleeping.

Rendering

Whatever currency we trade in,
whatever Caesar demands our fealty
c.o.d. in the coin of the realm,
his likeness stamped on a slug
of precious metal, clear enough
to frustrate counterfeiters,
we've still got to render unto God
in the coin bearing His image,
which is ourselves, which is more
than we can pay. Though we've tried
to deface ourselves, to debase
our currency, we can't erase
what we owe, only Christ can
satisfy, true likeness who surrendered
the new-minted coin of Himself.

For Example

Broad-veined, moss-furred, lichen-fringed,
eschewing the rhododendron's faux humility,
the evergreen's overstatement, and the indecisiveness
of the paper birch, the oak offers itself.
Ignoring the sky's blandishments
and the snow's accumulated ignorance,
radically committed to elemental truths,
it feeds on darkness yet lives in the light,
knows its place yet changes, season
by season becoming more like itself.

Extravagance

That woman never did know
when to quit, always too eager
to please, always too free
with her treasure, no sense
of propriety or value, a whole
year's wages wasted. Just think
it took a thousand flowers
to produce a single drop,
each one crushed to express
its essential oil, each drop
caught to fill that jar, one
would have been enough
for any man, but she
broke that alabaster jar
and poured it all upon his head.

So charged her critics,
champions of custom
and common sense
who, in a room filled
with fragrance and Christ,
thought of nothing
but cash, camouflaging
their indifference
to beauty and pleasure
as conscience.

He called them out on their false
concern for the poor, their impoverished

[handwritten margin note: Thought we were taking a sexual turn.]

[handwritten margin note: Mary at the feet of Jesus]

sense of occasion and praised her.
Ready to waste himself
without reservation, to be crushed,
his inexpressible love expressed
drop by drop, precious vessel broken
priceless blood poured out.

YES!

New Communion

Whoever bakes our bread makes it sweet.
I chew my piece and wish for a whole slice—
buttered, with coffee—think of Ezekiel,
God's word turning to honey on his tongue.

What a shock last Sunday to pop that rough cube
and taste salt, mouthing that tangy dough
to remember how sweet salvation was
bought with Christ's bitter suffering.

Tattoos

Clearly a matter of commitment.
And clearly I don't trust myself
to stay true to whatever image
or identity might inspire me.
My father, Semper Fi, bore his
Marine Corps emblem with pride.
At the pool my sisters and I
would trace that globe and anchor
which time finally reduced to a green
blur on his bicep but still there
beneath his suit when he received
his twenty-one gun salute.
As a teen I dreamed of an eagle
emblazoned on my chest,
to pull it off would have taken more
brawn and bronze than I possessed.
These days, though not quite tame,
there's no shame and so much more
to choose than skulls and snakes
or spider webs across the face.
I've seen the damasked arms
of athletes, collegiate bohemians
with crosses and geometric curiosities,
and the butterflies on soccer moms
showing off their wild side.
What if the ink I choose today
goes the way of my concert shirts,
dragon belt buckle, and long hair?
Who needs an epidermal palimpsest

of selves you no longer own
like the cartoon sailor with his arrowed
heart followed by a list of names
each crossed off except the last?
True, you can have a tat removed,
though it takes a knife to undo
the needle's work, acid, or laser
and maybe a graft to render
your skin blank and smooth.
I think I'll wait till the last day
let Jesus ink His name on a heart
set free from change, knowing
I can finally be always faithful.

Vegetables from my Neighbors' Gardens

They come as gifts,
green beans and broccoli,
yellow squash, zeppelin-like
zucchini, sun-ripened
tomatoes, cucumbers with thin
waxy skins and ears
of corn like silky-haired
papooses in green blankets,
things to slice, to sauté
in olive oil with onion
and garlic, the full flavor
of freshness, nothing canned
or frozen, nothing picked
unripe and shipped long
distances, no cellophane
or chemicals designed
to deliver what we want
whenever we want it.

They come as reminders
of my youth, the rototiller
gnawing the clay-rich soil,
stake and string lining
out the rows of lettuce
and beets and Swiss chard,
musk of tomato as I tied
the vines to splintery poles
with strips of terry cloth
towel, the cool summer

mornings when I hoed row
after row, the dew-soaked
leaves sprinkling my ankles.

They come as testimony
of our dependence
on the seasons, the alchemy
of sun and soil and rain
falling like grace
that to accept what's given
is not to give up
but to receive a gift.

Blessed

My wife's follow-up mammogram turned out
clear as the summer sky. In the easement

tulip poplars drip their sap, sticky
as the honey on our morning toast.

In his garden, my neighbor's beans
climb their poles and the tomato vines offer

their tributes to the sunshine.
Amidst the stiff current, the trout

hold themselves in place, and the placid deer
browse the underbrush. I'm grateful

for a life ordinary as a cornfield, abundant
and whole as my wife's breasts.

after Todd Davis

V

Icon Writing

Icon Writing

More than mechanical
reproduction or duplication
by a skilled copyist,
more than painting
from memory or model,
it is a discipline,
spiritual and artistic.

The materials matter,
of course, and the method
is prescribed by tradition
which is more than habit
but what's been proven
best for opening the visible
toward the invisible.
Each stroke proceeds
from prayer, each line
comes after contemplation
not the artist's usual
consideration of space
but his whole being
gathering itself
the way the pearl
of vision grows around
a grain of sand.

The result's not to be
looked at but through
and you are not

voyeur but voyager
ready to cross
into realms unknown.

Doors of Perception

This Mary's chunky and squat,
her curly-haired Christ sports
a Buddha belly and skeletal feet,
a fat gospel rests in his left hand,
his right gives the standard sign
of blessing, his face is
a flat-nosed grimace
without comeliness or grace.
Michael and Gabriel peer
round Mary's shoulders
like some backup duo,
tight coiffed, toga wearing,
their necks arced sideways
as if caught mid doo wop.

Such too-cute flippancy,
neither fresh nor accurate,
is far from spiritually operant,
although it's meant to free
my mind from piety
my tongue from habit
to help me see anew,
not to treat the image
as an inkblot but a door
whose panels I can press
to release the hidden catch.

But nothing springs. I feel
the lips forming to spew.
Fan me, O angel of zeal, fan me.

At the Burning Bush

Resting his left foot on the rock
as he loosens his sandal,
Moses has already heard the voice,
has already seen the red buds
resting on the bush's twiggy skeleton,
his nose, large and slightly bent,
seems to test the breeze,
his brow is barely wrinkled yet,
though his brooding eyes bear
a look that's difficult to read.

Does he see beyond this moment
with its strange promise of flame?
The plagues melting Pharaoh's
iron heart, the scorching desert,
pillar of fire, manna falling
like ash, quail thick as smoke,
the serpents' fiery tongues,
the smoldering wrath that finally
bloomed, consuming his chance
to enter the Promised Land?

Christmas Card Icon

This brown-robed Mary
bends her haloed head
over baby Jesus, swaddled
tight as a white pupa,
young and on the make.
Like hours on a clock face,
the usual suspects ring
the central pair, hardly
worth a second look
except for two surprises:
a midwife pours a bath
to wash away the scurf
of this very human birth,
and a Sasquatch wannabe,
who looks like John the B
in a camel-hair shirt
but is Old Scratch himself,
tickles the ears of Joseph
who tilts his head politely
but keeps his gown tucked
tightly round his knees,
a lime green carapace
impervious to hirsute lies.

Mothers and Sons

What mother love she must have shown
for her faithful son to dedicate
this fresco to her, the Widow Turtura.
What a comfort it must have been
to have his care and be included
in this holy scene, a dark-robed figure,
gaunt-faced, pale, and masculine.

How different from Mary, *Theotokos*,
who sits upon a "jewel-studded throne"
holding her golden child who blithely floats
on the purple cloud that is her robe.
His fleshy limbs and bulging belly
belie his too-small head and eyes
that look to heaven. Mary's don't.
She looks at you attentively
like a homely girl who hopes to please,
content to let this moment last
and keep her child in her arms.

Her fingers clasp a handkerchief
to clean her baby's cheek, perhaps,
or dab her dainty lips, or someday
wipe the tears of mother grief.

Crying in the Wilderness

Among the oldest icons in existence.
It looks it. Its colors and figures
have run and so much paint's
worn away you can see
the wood's vertical grain.
John's honey-colored nimbus is tattered,
and he's certainly decreased,
leaving much to the imagination
to figure out or fill in.
According to scholars, his scroll
once read, "Behold the Lamb
of God, which taketh away
the sins of the world."
Barely visible, his right hand
points toward a largely blurred
medallion of Christ.
He, too, seems to have decreased:
first-century rabbi, Palestinian
peasant whose real identity
and message were obscured,
some scholars claim,
by layer upon layer of lies
his disciples built up
and stylized. Nowadays
we've scraped our way
to the unvarnished truth.
Is that why John looks so sad?

He seems to say, "Lamb of God,
Christ, cousin, I am
still pointing your way."   NICE

The Business of Icons

My boss just bought an icon for his office,
a modest, Bible-toting, bald St. Paul.
A wax seal on the back attests that it's
been priestly blessed, an object fit for devotion,
a sticker verifies it's ISO compliant,
a dually certified commodity,
ready for the exchange of matter and spirit.

Favorite Saint

What should I do with this icon?
It's so old the paint's chipped in spots
and the whole thing's dark, composed
of mellow browns and tarnished gold,
some off-white highlights in the clothes,
though the painter's not forgot the body,
hid beneath that light-brushed robe,
the sunburned athlete's neck swelling the tunic.

Gripped in his left fist a slender rod,
cross-shaped, of course,
in his right a bouquet of three
black stems—keys to the kingdom.
His battered nimbus reminds us
beneath the heavenly overlay
lies earthy wood.

Face blotched like skin cancer
or large, brown tears,
right eye mostly gone
as if plucked to free you
from some earthly bond
or scraped away by sorrows
you couldn't stand to see,
while the left remains,
large, brown, clear,
and seems to follow me
whichever way I lean,
mouth closed, lips firm,

perhaps the look Christ gave
when the rooster crowed—
what, Peter, what did I do?

Man of Sorrows

How strong Mary must be
to hold the Christ so easily
or how light his infant body
as if he's yet to feel
the earth's full weight
like spring's first leaves
more sunlight than soil.

Tall and thin as a model,
clad in a tassel-fringed robe
and wimpled hood that frames
her smooth face and tender
look, she lets Christ float
in the bend of her arm, his left
hand grips a scroll, his right
gives a two-fingered salute
of peace, beneath his arched
brows his eyes are raised
to heaven, while Mary gazes
at the middle distance, her slender
fingers seem to say, "Behold!"
proud mother, premier witness.

I do not want that Christ.
I'd rather hold the one
full grown and wholly God,
who touched Judean dust,
knew hunger's pinch, the press
of wood against his neck,

who felt sin's deadly weight
before he grew so light
that he could rise again.

But I can't hold that Christ.
My arms lack Mary's strength,
my eyes her steady sight.
How much better it would be
if Christ took hold of me.

At the Cross

My but this panel is busy.
The artist, experiencing "*horror
vacui,*" has crowded the scene.

Golgotha looks like a cummerbund
decorated with flowers and the pale
Halloween skull of Adam.

The soldiers with their ornate shields
squat at the foot of the cross, clutching
thin spears and fingering Christ's tunic.

Overhead a quartet of diminutive
angels floats in the golden sky
their mouths flexed in a heavenly O.

From beneath Christ's armpit
a dotted line of blood arcs
into a small, two-handled jug.

He is flanked by the usual
suspects: two weeping women,
his mother and another Mary,

John, Bible in hand,
and the centurion, his new
faith indicated by his nimbus.

Like the artist of this golden ground

I, too, have a *"horror vacui"*
and crowd my mind with figures.

Sometimes like those mini angels
I hover above the earth, lip-syncing
songs of pure spirit.

Others I squat on the grass,
back to the cross, casting lots
for the world's seamless garment.

Or clad in saintly dress, I huddle
near but keep my eyes averted
like the Marys, dabbing tears,

or Bible-laden John who stares
at Jesus' knee. I would be
like the centurion, who knows

a human death and recognizes
the divine, a working soldier
with his eyes on Jesus' face
and his tongue ready to confess.

Breath

The gold frame holds the olive stone,
it holds the angel carved there, holds
the robes as straight and stiff as drapes,
the wings that hang like strips of cloth,
their gilt intact though growing faint.

Far from faint, my guilt still spreads.
Like a fine gold pollen, it coats
my driveway and deckchairs, it dusts
my doorknob and keyboard, gets trapped
in my trouser cuffs and fingernails.

It stains my wife's pale face and taints
our every kiss, it permeates
our pillow talk, its yellow cloud
has cast a shadow on my dreams.
What darkened blossom will it bring?

What unbending angel may appear
whose hollow eyes will hold me in
contempt, whose rigorous silence shout
my doom but will not stir a wing
to lift me up or wipe my tears?

I need a heart of flesh that feels
this pain, a tear-flushed face that knows
my flaws but will not leave me frozen,
whose breath can revive my jaded limbs
and burst the frame that holds them in.

Still Life

Forty martyrs who followed Christ
all the way to a cold grave,
frozen in bas relief whose stillness
still conveys their agony.

Naked from the waist up, their muscled
torsos contort against the cold,
their arms are clenched across their chests
or raised in supplication to Christ,
enthroned, three angels on each side
with draperied bodies still bent in worship.

Imagine how they must have trembled
when immersed in icy water, spastic
at first, their limbs numbing, their brown
skin pale then blue, their blood withdrawn,
and one by one their systems down,
heart beat slow, slower, stopped.
An indelicate death, so delicately carved.

Forty martyrs who will follow Christ,
their bodies rising on the last day,
their bulging calves and sculpted pecs
free from the still, cold clutch of ivory death.

Notes

"Icon writing" is a phrase often used for the process of painting or producing icons. Many of the poems in the "Icon Writing" section are responses to icons reproduced in Kurt Weitzmann, *The Icon: Holy Images—Sixth to Fourteenth Century* (New York: George Braziller, 1978).

"Doors of Perception": Plate 3, Berlin, Ivory Diptych with Christ and the Virgin

"At the Burning Bush": Plate 18, Sinai, Icon with Moses Before the Burning Bush

"Christmas Card Icon": "The Nativity of Our Lord" by the hand of Michael Kapeluck

"Mothers and Sons": Plate 5, Rome, Fresco with Virgin Enthroned, Flanked by Saint Felix and Saint Adauctus

"Crying in the Wilderness": Plate 7, Kiev, Encaustic Icon with St. John the Baptist

"Favorite Saint": Plate 8, Sinai, Encaustic Icon with Saint Peter

"Man of Sorrows": Plate 12, Utrecht, Ivory with Standing Virgin

"At the Cross": Plate 16, Munich, Enamel with Crucifixion

"Breath": Plate 13, Fiesole, Stealite with Archangel Gabriel

"Still Life": Plate 11, Berlin, Ivory with the Forty Martyrs of Sebast

26646699R00051

Made in the USA
San Bernardino, CA
02 December 2015